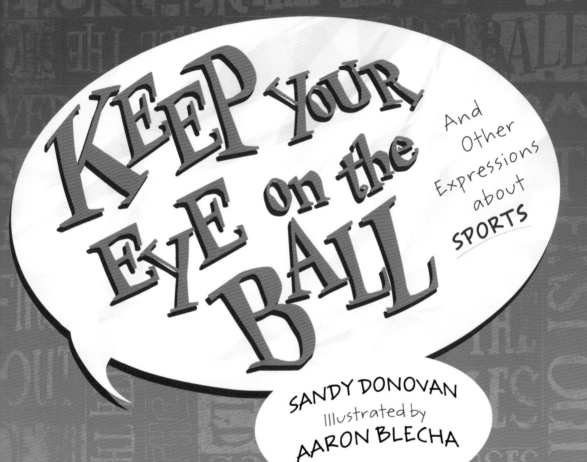

KEEP YOUR EYE on the BALL

And Other Expressions about SPORTS

SANDY DONOVAN

Illustrated by
AARON BLECHA

Lerner Publications Company
MINNEAPOLIS

Lerner Publications Company
A division of Lerner Publishing Group, Inc.
241 First Avenue North
Minneapolis, MN 55401 U.S.A.

Website address: www.lernerbooks.com

Library of Congress Cataloging-in-Publication Data

Donovan, Sandra, 1967–
    Keep your eye on the ball : and other expressions
  about sports / by Sandy Donovan.
      p.   cm. — (It's just an expression)
  Includes index.
  ISBN 978–0–7613–7889–1 (lib. bdg. : alk. paper)
    1. English language—Idioms—Juvenile literature.
  2. Sports—Juvenile literature. I. Title.
  PE1460.D66 2013
  428.1—dc23   9262   2011044705

Manufactured in the United States of America
1 – PC – 7/15/12

TABLE of CONTENTS

INTRODUCTION

So you're hanging out one day, feeling like you've got **all your bases covered**. But **out of left field**, your best friend starts picking a fight with you. You try to stay calm, even **roll with the punches**, but boy, it's hard to defend yourself. You know **the ball's in your court**, and you can work everything out with him in the end as long as you don't strike out.

What the heck is happening in the scenario above?! Nothing you can't figure out if you get clued into the world of idioms. Idioms are phrases that mean something different from what you might think they mean. A lot of common idioms come from phrases in sports. When used in everyday life, these phrases can seem crazy confusing. But once you learn what idioms mean (and where on earth they came from), they're not so confusing after all. So check them out, and soon you'll be **calling all the shots**.

COVER Your BASES

Jin's dad tells him that he needs to cover all his bases. But they're talking about studying for a math test, so Jin isn't sure what his dad means.

When he asks, his dad says that *cover your bases* means "be prepared for anything that may happen." He tells Jin he should study everything his class has covered so far in math, because he never knows what will pop up on the test.

Still, Jin can't help thinking that maybe his dad is sending him a secret message. Maybe his dad really wants him to forget about math and go play some baseball. After all, nobody covers bases like a good infield baseball player.

Jin is partly right. Not about his dad—he really does want Jin to study. But Jin is right that the expression "cover your bases" comes from baseball. When playing infield, players stand next to a base so they can be prepared to catch any ball and tag a runner out.

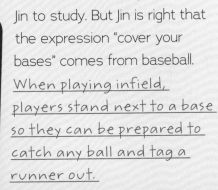

SAVED by the BELL

"Saved by the Bell, Mariah," said Ms. Lee. Just when Mariah's teacher had asked her to explain a math problem, the end-of-class bell rang. A huge piece of luck—since Mariah had no idea how to do the problem.

Lots of people use the expression *saved by the bell* to mean getting out of something unpleasant by being interrupted. And for kids, the end-of-class bell is the most common bell to be saved by.

But this expression doesn't really come from school bells. It's a boxing term, and it's been around since boxing became popular in the early 1900s. When boxers get knocked down, they have ten seconds to get back on their feet. A referee counts the seconds out loud. If the boxer isn't up by the count of ten, he or she loses the fight. However, there's one way a boxer can gain a little extra time to recover.

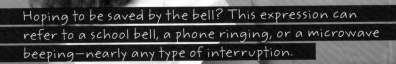

Hoping to be saved by the bell? This expression can refer to a school bell, a phone ringing, or a microwave beeping—nearly any type of interruption.

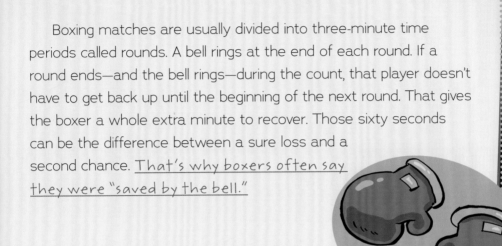

Boxing matches are usually divided into three-minute time periods called rounds. A bell rings at the end of each round. If a round ends—and the bell rings—during the count, that player doesn't have to get back up until the beginning of the next round. That gives the boxer a whole extra minute to recover. Those sixty seconds can be the difference between a sure loss and a second chance. That's why boxers often say they were "saved by the bell."

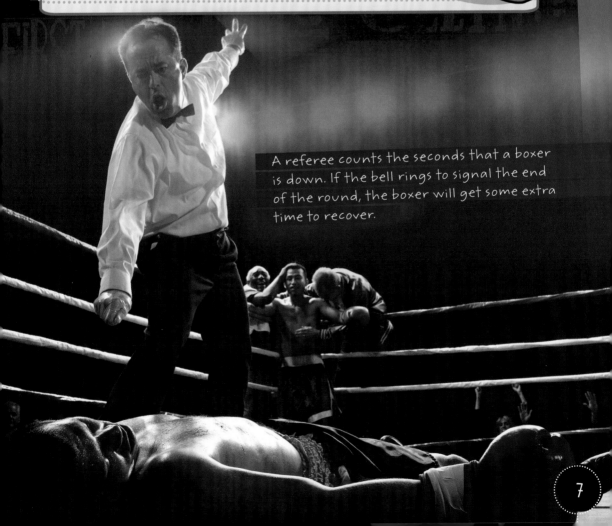

A referee counts the seconds that a boxer is down. If the bell rings to signal the end of the round, the boxer will get some extra time to recover.

DROP the BALL

When Emma's mom told her she really dropped the ball this time, Emma knew that wasn't a good thing. She was supposed to have her room cleaned up by the time her mom got home from work. But by 6:00, when her mom walked into their apartment, Emma's room was still a disaster.

So what happened? Did Emma make the mess even worse by dropping a ball in her room? No! **Drop the ball is just an expression that means to make a mistake by being careless.** Emma just forgot about her deadline, and so she missed it. Instead of cleaning her room, she got distracted by her cell phone. This expression comes from football. Dropping the ball is one of the worst mistakes you can make in football. It's called a fumble, and it can give the other team a chance to gain control of the ball and even score points.

There's one dropped ball that's so famous in football history, it's simply called the Fumble. The Fumble happened on January 17, 1988, in the American Football Conference Championship game between the Cleveland Browns and the Denver Broncos. With one minute and twelve seconds left in the game, the Browns were losing by one touchdown. Browns running back Earnest Byner had the ball and was nearing a touchdown. At the two-yard line, he dropped the ball. The Broncos recovered the fumble, won the game, and went on to the Super Bowl.

A teammate comforts Earnest Byner (44) of the Browns after Byner fumbled in the last two minutes of the AFC Championship game.

OUT of LEFT FIELD

"Wow, that really came out of left field," Francis told Zoe.

Zoe didn't know what he meant—and really, she didn't care. Their teacher had just told them they could go outside and play instead of taking their spelling test! Who had time to ponder what Francis said?

Was Francis talking about playing on the school's left-side field? Not really. **Out of left field is an idiom that means something was really unexpected and odd.**

Most people agree that this common expression has its roots in baseball. But people have different opinions about what exactly *left field* refers to. Some people say it was first used to describe some confused fans who came to see the famous Yankees player Babe Ruth. From his first major-league game in

1914 to his last in 1935, Babe Ruth was the most popular baseball player in the country. He batted left-handed, so his home runs often soared above right field. He also played right field. Seats in right field became very popular. And out in left field was a way of describing the clueless fans who bought tickets in left field.

Some others claim that the expression refers to the left field at Chicago's West Side Park, the former home of the Chicago Cubs. That field was once home to the Neuropsychiatric Institute of the University of Illinois, which studies and treats mental health disorders. Some say being "in left field" came to mean having such a disorder.

Babe Ruth stands in the outfield at Yankee Stadium in 1925.

The BALL's in YOUR COURT

Jayden's mom told him that the ball is in his court. But he's stuck in his room without a ball in sight. She told him to stay there while he thinks about how he started a fight with his sister. If he wants his freedom back, he'll have to apologize to his sister. So why is his mom talking about a ball?

*T*he **ball's in your court is another way of saying that it's your turn to make the next move.** Jayden's mom is telling him that it's up to him to fix things. If he apologizes to his sister, he can get back to playing. If he doesn't, he'll probably be stuck in his room for the rest of the day.

This expression could apply to a lot of sports that are played on courts. Basketball, racquetball, and tennis all include balls and courts. But most people agree that "the ball's in your court" was first used in tennis games in the second half of the 1900s. In tennis, everything on your side of the net is your court. On the other side of the net is your opponent's court. You hit the ball over the net to your opponent, and he or she hits it back to you. When the ball's in your court, it's your chance to make a move. Hopefully your move will be to hit the ball back over the net to keep the game going!

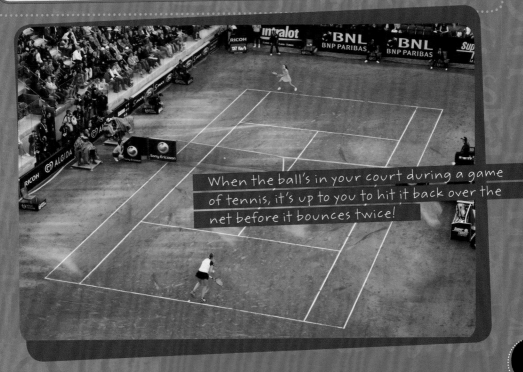

When the ball's in your court during a game of tennis, it's up to you to hit it back over the net before it bounces twice!

PULL Your PUNCHES

May's older brother said she sure doesn't pull any punches. When you ask May what she thinks, she tells you exactly what's on her mind.

Pull her punches? Why would she be punching at all if her brother just wants to know what she thinks? And what does pulling have to do with anything?

May isn't really doing any punching—or pulling, for that matter. **Pulling your punches is an expression that means you are holding back.** It can also mean dealing with things in a dishonest way.

Watch out—this boxer doesn't pull her punches!

Sparring partners practice their boxing moves on each other. They might pull their punches so they don't hurt their partner.

This expression comes from boxing. It may have been used as early as the 1800s, when some of the first modern boxing matches took place in England. When a boxer pulls punches, he or she holds back some strength. The opponent isn't hit as hard. It's common for boxers to do this when they're sparring, or practicing. It softens the blow and keeps them from hurting their practice partner. Sounds civilized, right?

Sometimes boxers pull their punches in real matches too. They might even do this out of compassion, or kindness toward an opponent. Again, it sounds civilized. But pulling punches is illegal in professional boxing. It can be used as a way to throw a game, or allow an opponent to win. And doing that is against the rules in just about any sport.

CLEAR the HURDLES

"Only one more hurdle to clear before the end of the school year!" Maya announced. She finished her social studies report. She took her last math test. All she has left to do is turn in her book report.

So why is she thinking about clearing hurdles? Shouldn't she be focusing on her report? What she really means is that she's made it through several difficult tasks and that she has one more left to reach her goal.

This expression probably comes from a track-and-field event called the hurdle race, practiced in England since the 1830s. In a hurdle race, runners have to leap over a series of obstacles called hurdles. But the phrase might also come from the much older sport of horse racing. Many horse racing events have hurdles. The hurdles can be made out of wood, plastic, or metal. Most events feature ten hurdles placed at equal distances from one another along the race course. Jumping over them without falling down is tricky for both runners and horses. <u>So when you clear a hurdle—or successfully jump over it—you're one step closer to the goal of winning it all.</u> Of course, to win, you have to not just clear all the hurdles—you have to do it in the fastest time too. Maya thinks maybe she'll stick to report writing.

Some of the world's top female athletes compete in a 110-meter (361 feet) hurdle race.

TWO STRIKES

"That's two strikes," Sydney's dad told her. "Do you want to try for a third?" Sydney knows she's in trouble, but she's not sure why her dad is talking about strikes. What's a third strike exactly, and would a third strike get her in more or less trouble?

After she thinks about it, she can tell by the look on her dad's face that she doesn't want to find out what a third strike would mean.

If Sydney were a baseball player, she'd know that you get three strikes before you're out. **So when Sydney's dad warns her that she has two strikes, he's saying that she has only one more chance before she's in really, really big trouble.**

<u>Interestingly, there's one sport where three strikes is a good thing.</u> In bowling, a strike means that you knock down all ten pins with one ball. When you get three strikes in one game, it's called a turkey. It's a rare and exciting accomplishment. Hmm, maybe Sydney should ask her dad if he's talking about baseball or bowling. On second thought, he doesn't look like he's in the mood for questions.

Adam Dunn, of the Chicago White Sox, swings and gets a strike. One strike is no biggie. But two strikes and you're cutting it close, and three strikes and you're out.

KEEP Your EYE on the BALL

Mason's dad encouraged him to keep his eye on the ball. But they weren't talking about baseball, football, or basketball. They were just talking about Mason's bank account!

Keeping your eye on the ball means "staying focused on your goal." People have used the expression since about 1900 to remind themselves not to get distracted by the small things. If you let yourself lose focus, after all, you might not meet your goal. And Mason's goal is to save $200 before the end of summer. To do that, he has to mow *a lot* of lawns. So even though Mason is getting really tired of mowing lawns, he'll keep on doing it. And he'll keep his eye on the ball—or, rather, on his bank account.

In tennis, keeping your eye on the ball helps you hit it with the racket just the right way.

This expression can apply to almost any sport, but it most likely comes from tennis or baseball. In those games especially, players need to carefully watch the path of the ball. If they lose sight of the ball, they can miss an important chance. A tennis player can miss a return hit, a baseball batter can miss a ball, and an outfielder can flub a crucial catch. And any of those mistakes can keep a player—or a team—from reaching their ultimate goal of winning the game.

ROLL with the PUNCHES

Alex's uncle told him that sometimes you need to roll with the punches. Alex doesn't think he means rolling around on the floor. And he doesn't think he was talking about punching anybody either.

Alex is right. **Roll with the punches is another way of saying, "Don't take things too hard."**

In fact, Alex has been having a rough time lately. His best friend moved away last month. Then today he found out he couldn't go to the summer camp he wanted to go to. His uncle is telling him to try to look past these disappointments. He thinks Alex will be happier if he thinks less about unhappy events and more about happy events. To get past disappointments, people often say they need to "roll with the punches."

This expression comes from boxing. When a boxer gets hit, he or she tries to roll with the punch. This means the boxer moves smoothly away from the hit. This softens the blow and causes the boxer less pain—which means he or she has more energy left to continue the fight. So a boxer who can roll with the punches is usually more successful in the ring—just as a person who can roll with life's punches is often more successful and happy.

The boxer on the left rolls away from the punch he's taking. Luckily, "rolling with the punches" for most people is less painful than this!

CALL the SHOTS

Antwon's mom told him that he does not call the shots around their house. And Antwon, who almost always has plenty to say, has no idea what to say to this. What is she talking about, calling the shots?

Call the shots is an idiom that means "being in control." The person who calls the shots is the person who decides what's going to happen. So Antwon's mom is saying that Antwon isn't in control—he doesn't make the decisions at his house. Antwon guesses she didn't appreciate his saying he should get to watch his favorite show whenever he wants.

Calling your shot in pool lets the other player know which pocket you're aiming for. But if you hit a ball into a different pocket, you might lose your turn.

<u>People have different ideas about where this idiom comes from.</u> Many people say it comes from billiards or pool. These games are played with long cue sticks, numbered balls, and a table with pockets to shoot the balls into. Players have to announce where they are aiming in advance of their turn. So they study their options and decide what would be their best play. Then they might call out, "Two ball in the corner pocket."

Others believe that this idiom got started with the sport of target shooting. In target shooting, the shooter sometimes announces where the target will be hit. Other times, someone else "calls the shots" and gives orders to the shooter about where to aim. In either case, the person calling the shots is the person making decisions.

FIRST out of the GATE

"I want to be first out of the gate when recess finally gets here," James whispers to Chen as their teacher passes out an assignment.

Huh? Is there *really* a gate between the classroom and the school playground? Of course not. James just wants to be one of the first kids out the door and on the playground. **That's all *first out of the gate* means—"to be the first to get somewhere."**

The expression *first out of the gate* comes from horse racing. When horses are getting ready to run a race, they line up behind a gate. When the gate is raised, the race is on. All the horses push to

get out first. You can probably picture a bunch of kids trying to race out to the playground—they might look a lot like a bunch of horses rushing onto the racetrack.

Sometimes people use this expression without the word *first*. For instance, a teacher might say, "James always runs to the basketball court out of the gate." This idiom also comes from horse racing, and it means "at the start." You can probably guess why: the horses go out of the gate at the very beginning of a race.

Jockeys and their horses rush out of the gate at the beginning of a race in Russia.

A SCREWBALL

"Eliot, you're such a screwball," said Jackson. Eliot's heard that before. Everyone says he's a screwball—his mom, his dad, his teachers, and even his best friends, like Jackson!

Eliot doesn't have much to do with screws or balls. But he does do crazy, zany things. A lot of them, in fact.

Calling someone a screwball is another way of saying that they are unusual, wacky, loony, crazy, nutty ... well, you get the idea. Screwballs do odd and funny things.

The expression comes from a famous baseball pitch called—you guessed it—the screwball. <u>This is a slightly odd pitch that was made famous in the early 1900s by a player named Christy Mathewson.</u> The screwball does the unexpected. It starts out like a curveball. That's a pitch that veers, or quickly curves, after it's thrown. A curveball veers to the left when it's thrown by a right-handed pitcher. And it veers to the right when it's thrown by a left-handed pitcher.

But a screwball does just the opposite. Just when a batter expects a ball to curve one way, a screwball curves the other way. It's a great pitch because it confuses batters most of the time. Unfortunately, it's also very tough on a pitcher's arm. Pitchers don't throw many screwballs so that they don't injure their arms.

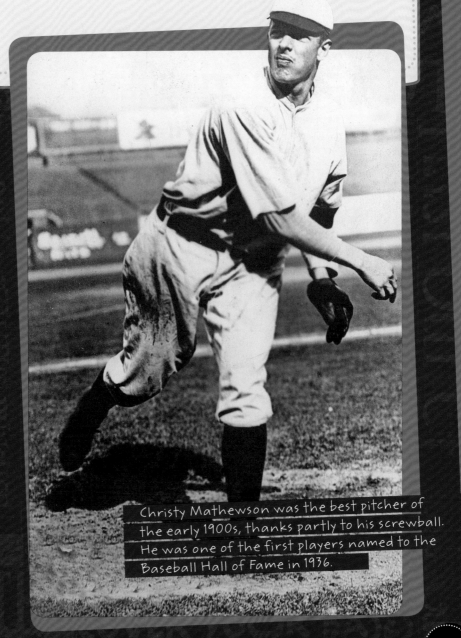

Christy Mathewson was the best pitcher of the early 1900s, thanks partly to his screwball. He was one of the first players named to the Baseball Hall of Fame in 1936.

Glossary

American Football Conference: one of the two conferences that make up the National Football League (NFL)

compassion: sympathy for the suffering of others

flub: to mess something up

fumble: to drop or mishandle a ball in football

hurdle: a barrier that a runner or a horse jumps over in a race

idiom: a commonly used expression or phrase that means something different from what it appears to mean

infield: the area of a baseball field between home plate and the three bases

ponder: to think about something carefully

professional: getting paid to do a job or to perform in a sport

referee: the official who oversees a sports contest and enforces the rules

sparring: a practice boxing match

veer: to change direction

zany: unusual in an amusing way

Further Reading

Bhall, Jag. *I'm Not Hanging Noodles on Your Ears and Other Intriguing Idioms from around the World.* New York: National Geographic, 2009.
Did you know that in Russian "I'm not hanging noodles on your ears" means "I'm telling you the truth"? Learn more wacky idioms from cultures around the globe in this amusing collection.

Doeden, Matt. *Stick Out Like a Sore Thumb: And Other Expressions about Body Parts.* Minneapolis: Lerner Publications Company, 2013.
Find out the real meaning of expressions involving thumbs and other body parts through this book's funny text and wacky illustrations.

Gray, Ryan. *The Language of Baseball: A Complete Dictionary of Slang Terms, Clichés, and Expressions from the Grand Ole Game.* Monterey, CA: Coaches Choice Publishers, 2002.
Learn about the wealth of terms and expressions inspired by the game of baseball in this encyclopedia-like book.

Heos, Bridget. *Cool as a Cucumber: And Other Expressions about Food.* Minneapolis: Lerner Publications Company, 2013.
Enjoy more of Aaron Blecha's artwork with explanations of *in a pickle, bring home the bacon,* and other food-related idioms.

Idioms by Kids
http://www.idiomsbykids.com
Check out more than one thousand kid-drawn pictures of the literal meanings of idioms! You can add your own examples too.

Idiom Site
http://www.idiomsite.com
Search this alphabetical list of idioms and their meanings.

Paint by Idioms
http://www.funbrain.com/idioms
Test your knowledge of common idioms by taking the multiple-choice quizzes on this site from FunBrain.com.

Terban, Marvin. *Scholastic Dictionary of Idioms.* Rev. ed. New York: Scholastic, 2006.
Look up explanations for more than seven hundred idioms in this reference book with alphabetical listings and an index.

LERNER
SOURCE
Expand learning beyond the printed book. Download free, complementary educational resources for this book from our website, www.lernerresource.com.

Index

Photo Acknowledgments

The images in this book are used with the permission of: © JGI/Tom Grill/Blend Images/Getty Images, p. 5; © FancyVeerSet1/Fancy/Alamy, p. 6; © Mike Powell/ The Image Bank/Getty Images, p. 7; © B2M Productions/Digital Visions/Getty Images, p. 8; AP Photo/Mark Duncan, p. 9; © Fuse/Getty Images, p. 10; © Mark Rucker/Transcendental Graphics/Getty Images, p. 11; © Jamie Grill/Iconica/Getty Images, p. 12; © Alessandro0770/Dreamstime.com, p. 13; © imagebroker.net/ SuperStock, p. 14; Zuma Press/Newscom, p. 15; © Geri Lavrov/Photographer's Choice/Getty Images, p. 16; © Hector Guerrero/AFP/Getty Images, p. 17; © JGI/ Jamie Grill/Blend Images/Getty Images, p. 18; © Ron Vesely/MLB Photos via Getty Images, p. 19; © iStockphoto.com/-Oxford-, p. 21; © Stockbyte/Getty Images, p. 22; © Nicholas Piccillo/Shutterstock.com, p. 23; © Wavebreakmedia ltd/Shutterstock.com, p. 25; © Matt Henry Gunther/Stone/Getty Images, p. 26; © Mikhail Pogosov/Shutterstock.com, p. 27; © FPG/Archive Photos/Getty Images, p. 29.

Front cover: AP Photo/Carolyn Kaster, (boy); © Brodogg1313/Dreamstime.com, (stands); © Todd Strand/Independent Picture Service, (baseball).

Main body text set in Adrianna Light 11/17.
Typeface provided by Chank.